WHO WAS BORN AT HOME?

BY CORIE FEINER   ILLUSTRATED BY GEORGE SANDIDGE

FOUR STEPS PRESS
New York, NY

For Buster
born "right here."
C.F.

For my mother
who was born at home.
G.S.

WHO WAS BORN AT HOME?

BY CORIE FEINER   ILLUSTRATED BY GEORGE SANDIDGE

**In a little log cabin with a dry dirt floor
on Sinking Spring Farm's soft red loam**

**Abraham Lincoln
was born at home.**

**In a red brick house on a hill
before the electric lamp or the telephone**

**Thomas Edison
was born at home.**

**On 37th Street in New York City
in an apartment above the traffic's drone**

**Eleanor Roosevelt
was born at home.**

**In a wood-frame cottage on a high bluff
before the morning flag was flown**

**Amelia Earhart
was born at home.**

Up six wobbly steps and a splintered porch
in a plywood shanty that stood alone

**Rosa Parks
was born at home.**

In a brown frame house on Auburn Avenue
in a room upstairs in the evening's gloam

**Martin Luther King, Jr.
was born at home.**

**In a hand-built shack of two small rooms
lit with oil lamps of nickel and chrome**

**Elvis Presley
was born at home.**

In cabins, apartments, and houses of stone,

babies have been born among sweet cries and moans.

**And right here, my dear one,
now it is known, that you my dear child,**

were born at home.

Abraham Lincoln (1809-1865) was born on February 12,1809 on Sinking Spring Farm in Kentucky. Our 16th President of the United States, he succeeded in leading the country through the American Civil War and in ending slavery. He was a powerful speaker and his Gettysburg Address is one of the most quoted speeches in United States history.

Thomas Alva Edison (1847-1931) was born on February 11,1847 in Milan, Ohio. He was an inventor who invented a method of providing the general public with safe, stable, and efficient electric light and power for the first time in history! He also gave us the electric light bulb, the phonograph, the motion picture camera, the microphone and thousands of other devices that changed life for all of humanity.

Eleanor Roosevelt (1884-1962) was born on October 11, 1884 in New York City, New York. She was the wife of President Franklin D. Roosevelt and served as First Lady of the United States from 1933 to 1945. She showed the world that the first lady was an important part of American politics. Eleanor helped the country's poor and stood up for women, children, and equal rights for all.

Amelia Mary Earhart (1897-missing 1937; declared deceased 1939) was born on July 24, 1897 in Atchison, Kansas in the home of her maternal grandfather. She was the world's most famous female aviator. Amelia was the first woman, and the second person ever, to fly across the Atlantic Ocean, the first woman to fly solo nonstop coast to coast, and the first person to fly solo from Hawaii to California.

Rosa Parks (1913- 2005) was born Rosa Louise McCauley in Tuskegee, Alabama on February 4, 1913. She is nationally recognized as the "mother of the modern day civil rights movement" in America. Her refusal to give up her seat to a white male passenger on a Montgomery, Alabama bus in 1955, triggered a bus boycott by African-Americans, led by Reverend Martin Luther King,Jr. This eventually led to desegregation in Montgomery and elsewhere in the United States.

Martin Luther King, Jr. (1929-1968) was born on January 15, 1929 in Atlanta, Georgia. The leader of the United States civil rights movement, Dr. King promoted nonviolent direct action and led marches against segregation and racial discrimination. His famous "I Have a Dream" speech given at the Lincoln Memorial in Washington, D.C. led the U.S. Congress to more quickly pass the Civil Rights Act, giving African-Americans equal treatment. Dr. King won the Nobel Peace Prize in 1964.

Elvis Aaron Presley(1935-1977) was born on January 8, 1935 in East Tupelo, Mississippi. His career as a singer and entertainer redefined American popular music. Elvis starred in 33 successful films, made history with his television appearances and specials, and was known for his record-breaking live concerts. He has sold over one billion records worldwide, more than any other artist.

Text copyright © 2011 Corie Feiner
Illustrations copyright © 2011 by George Sandidge

Library of Congress Cataloging-in-Publication Data is available.

ISBN-13: 978-1456346232
ISBN-10: 1456346237

The book was typeset in Futura Medium.
The illustrations were done in Watercolor.

Four Steps Press
P.O. Box 231213
New York, NY 10023

CORIE FEINER was inspired to write, Who Was Born at Home? after the successful homebirth of her son. An award winning and widely published poet, she is the author of, Radishes into Roses. She lives in New York City with her husband and son. This is her first children's book.

GEORGE SANDIDGE received his masters in illustration from the Savannah College of Art and Design. His paintings have been featured in galleries in Savannah, in the Atlanta Journal Constitution and in American Artist: Watercolor magazine. He lives in the small town of Winnsboro, South Carolina within walking distance of the house were his mother and grandmother where born.

Made in the USA
Lexington, KY
08 January 2013